Operation Enduring Freedom

The War on Terrorism

By John Hamilton

Visit us at
www.abdopub.com

Published by ABDO & Daughters, an imprint of ABDO Publishing Company, 4940 Viking Drive, Suite 622, Edina, Minnesota 55435. Copyright ©2002 by Abdo Consulting Group, Inc. International copyrights reserved in all countries. No part of this book may be reproduced in any form without written permission from the publisher.

Printed in the United States.

Edited by Paul Joseph
Graphic Design: John Hamilton
Cover Design: Mighty Media
Photos: AP/Wide World, DoD

Library of Congress Cataloging-in-Publication Data

Hamilton, John 1959-
    Operation Enduring Freedom / John Hamilton.
      p. cm. — (War on terrorism)
    Includes index.
    Summary: Reviews the escalating actions of the United States in Afghanistan, using airstrikes and other tactics to eliminate the Taliban and its leader, Osama bin Laden, after the September 11, 2001 terrorist attacks.
    ISBN 1-57765-665-2
    1. Afghanistan—History—2001- —Juvenile literature. 2. War on terrorism, 2001- — Juvenile literature. [1. Afghanistan—History—2001-. 2. War on terrorism, 2001-.] I. Title. II. Series.

DS371.4.H36 2002
958.104'6—dc21

2001056725

Table of Contents

This AC-130 Spectre gunship is on a mission over Afghanistan. Note the red-tipped weapons projecting out the right side.

Fighting Spirit

A Marine Corps F/A-18C Hornet attack fighter flies past the American flag atop the bridge of the aircraft carrier USS Theodore Roosevelt.

America Strikes Back

N SEPTEMBER 11, 2001, THE FORCES OF terror struck at the very heart of the United States. Hijackers turned two jumbo jets into missiles, destroying New York City's World Trade Center. In Washington, D.C., another hijacked plane crashed into the Pentagon, the symbolic center of U.S. military power. A fourth jet, destination unknown, crashed into a farm field in rural Pennsylvania. It was almost certainly brought down by courageous passengers who chose to fight back rather than let the terrorists kill more people on the ground.

On that horrifying day, thousands of innocent civilians were killed or injured, victims of the worst terrorist attack ever on U.S. soil. Americans reacted with shock and anger. Most of all they wanted to know, who could do such a thing? Who was responsible? And when would the United States strike back?

On September 13, Secretary of State Colin Powell identified Osama bin Laden as the prime suspect in the attacks. Bin Laden, the leader of a terrorist network known as al-Qaeda (the Base), had been wanted by the U.S. since the October 2000 attack on the USS *Cole* in Yemen, and the 1998 bombings of the U.S. embassies in Tanzania and Kenya.

Arresting bin Laden and bringing him to justice was complicated because he lived in one of the most remote, hostile, and lawless countries in the world—Afghanistan. The central Asian nation had known nothing but war for nearly a quarter century. Its land was ruined, its cities were destroyed, and its people were desperate. Ruling over this land was a fundamentalist Islamic regime called the Taliban. The Taliban agreed with bin Laden's strict religious views; they were also happy to take the terrorist's money. In return, they protected him, letting him use Afghanistan as a base for his al-Qaeda terror network. After the September 11 attacks, the U.S. demanded that the Taliban turn over bin Laden. The Taliban refused.

On September 15, 2001, President Bush ordered the U.S. military to prepare for war. He gave a speech two days later, bracing the American people for a long and difficult struggle against the forces of terrorism. The president said that the armed forces of the United States would "defend freedom at any cost." He also said that Osama bin Laden was wanted by the U.S. "dead or alive."

On September 19, U.S. armed forces began sending troops, planes, and ships to the region surrounding Afghanistan, a sure sign that a military strike was near. The military operation was called Infinite Justice. Islamic scholars soon objected to the name, saying that only God could deliver infinite justice. Because the U.S. was trying hard to show the Islamic world that this was a war against terrorism, not Islam, the military changed the name to Operation Enduring Freedom on September 24.

By the last week of September, the Pentagon reported that Special Forces teams had been on scouting missions inside

Afghanistan. These missions, the military explained, were mainly carried out to identify likely targets for air strikes, although they were also part of the hunt for bin Laden.

Four aircraft carrier battle groups were soon in the region. The former Soviet republic of Uzbekistan, which borders Afghanistan to the north, allowed U.S. troops to use one of its air bases. This was important; it allowed U.S. forces to get close to the field of battle. The U.S. also used bases in Pakistan, which shares its western border with Afghanistan.

The U.S. military was ready to go. Diplomatically, key countries around the world backed the war against terrorism. All was prepared. By the first week of October 2001, the United States was ready to strike back.

Ambush In Afghanistan

Afghan soldiers shoot from protected hillsides at retreating British forces in 1842.

The Great Game

ECAUSE OF ITS LOCATION BETWEEN INDIA, Iran, and central Asia, Afghanistan has been invaded many times, suffering the ravages of war for several centuries. During the early 1800s, Britain and Russia competed for influence in central Asia. Britain was concerned that the Russians would attack the British colony of India. To keep control of the northern routes to India, the British installed a ruler in Afghanistan who was friendly to British interests. But the Afghan people fought against the British-supported government. This led to the Anglo-Afghan Wars. In Europe, where superior military technology made Afghanistan seem like an easy conquest, the operation was cynically known as the Great Game. To the Afghan people, it was yet another invasion of their homeland, which would bring years of misery and death.

At first, the British invasion of Afghanistan was successful. They took over the capital of Kabul and set up a government friendly to England. Things went downhill from there. During the last years of the war, Afghan guerrilla fighters decimated the British forces. The Afghans had the advantage of striking fast and then blending back into the safety of the rugged mountains.

On January 5, 1842, nearly 17,000 British troops, their families, and camp followers retreated, heading back to the safety of India. Along the way, Afghan fighters hiding in the surrounding hills fired on them. After a week of ruthless fighting, only a single Briton made it back to safety. It was one of the most humiliating defeats in British military history.

As the British discovered during their occupation, the Afghans are a fierce, tribal people skilled at defending their homeland, especially in the rugged mountain areas. In the next century, the Soviet Union would also learn this harsh lesson.

In 1979, the Soviet military was sent into Afghanistan to support the country's Communist government, which was under attack from a collection of tribal guerrilla fighters called the *mujahideen*. At first, just like the British before them, the Soviets succeeded in their invasion. Over time, however, the *mujahideen* attacks became more effective, and the civil war raged on.

Even after the Soviets sent in more than 100,000 troops, the two sides reached a stalemate. The *mujahideen* were being supplied with weapons by several Western nations, including the United States, which wanted the Soviet invasion to fail. Finally, in 1989, the last Soviet military forces withdrew from Afghanistan. It was a humiliating defeat for the Soviets, with severe consequences for years to come. (Many historians compare it to the U.S. experience in Vietnam.) Casualty estimates vary, but nearly 15,000 Soviet soldiers lost their lives, and more than 50,000 were wounded. More than 400,000 others became ill.

On the Afghan side, the toll was even more terrible. More than one million Afghans died, and another five million refugees were left scattered across the countryside, and in neighboring Pakistan and Iran. The cities of Afghanistan were left in ruins, the government was weak, and its army was ready to collapse.

Soviet Retreat

. A Soviet tank is one of the last units to cross from Afghanistan back into the USSR February 5, 1989.

The *mujahideen* continued battling what was left of the Communist government forces. By 1992, they claimed victory and occupied the capital of Kabul. But tribal bickering soon caused the shaky government to fall apart. Civil war continued until a group of radical Muslim fighters, called the Taliban, gathered enough weapons and popular support to take over.

Afghanistan's people were happy that the Taliban had restored law and order, but it would come with a heavy price. The Taliban interpreted the religion of Islam in the strictest way possible, and quickly imposed their views on the Afghan people. Women could no longer work or get an education. Men had to grow long beards. Children were forbidden to fly kites. The list of restrictions was long, and the Taliban enforced their rules by terrorizing the Afghan people. It was a harsh way of life, and those who disobeyed were severely punished, often with death.

Osama bin Laden was a Saudi Arabian citizen and millionaire who fought alongside the *mujahideen* during the Soviet invasion of Afghanistan. After the Soviets withdrew, bin Laden lived in Saudi Arabia and Sudan, until he was expelled because of his terrorist connections. By 1996, bin Laden had returned to Afghanistan, where he continued growing his al-Qaeda terror network.

Taliban In Control

Taliban fighters ride atop an armored personnel carrier north of the Afghan capital of Kabul.

Osama bin Laden was a Muslim radical who dreamed of a fundamental Islamic state that would rise up and destroy the countries of the West, especially the United States. The breakdown of the government in Afghanistan made the country an ideal home for al-Qaeda. He formed a strong alliance with the Taliban's leader, Mullah Mohammed Omar. They both had radical religious beliefs, coupled with a mania for power. Bin Laden gave the Taliban money and weapons to support their iron grip on the countryside. In return, bin Laden was free to build up his terror network, including training camps, without government interference. Protected by the Taliban, bin Laden and al-Qaeda grew into a worldwide menace.

After bin Laden was found responsible for the USS *Cole* and African embassy attacks, President Bill Clinton ordered cruise missile attacks against Afghan terrorist training camps. Damage was done, but there was no follow-up; the U.S. was unprepared for full-scale war and the American deaths that would surely follow.

Bin Laden saw this inaction as weakness. He prepared to carry out his most bold and terrifying attack yet. On September 11, 2001, New York and Washington, D.C., suffered the United States' worst terror attack ever, with thousands of innocent civilians killed. This time, the U.S. *had* to respond.

It was against this backdrop in 2001 that the United States prepared to destroy the Taliban regime and with it, Osama bin Laden's al-Qaeda terror network. The U.S. was mindful of the mistakes made by invading forces of the past. A full-scale invasion, like the U.S.-led 1991 Persian Gulf War against Iraq, could easily bring disaster in the treacherous hills of Afghanistan. What was needed was a new way to wage war.

Night Stalkers

A U.S. soldier, seen through a night-vision scope, guards an airstrip in Afghanistan.

The Tip Of The Spear

THE UNITED STATES HAD SEVERAL GOALS when it went to war in Afghanistan. First and foremost, Osama bin Laden and his al-Qaeda terror network had to be shut down. To get to al-Qaeda, the U.S. would have to destroy the ruling Taliban regime. Seizing information on the battlefield, such as computers and paper documents, would help U.S. investigators disrupt future terror attacks.

The U.S. also had a humanitarian crisis on its hands. Millions of Afghan refugees were scattered throughout the country. These people desperately needed food and other supplies, and the harsh Afghan winter was quickly approaching.

United Nations relief convoys had already sent shipments of food and supplies to refugee camps within Afghanistan, but they were now blocked by Taliban soldiers. To help ease the humanitarian crises, the U.S. began air-dropping thousands of meal packets and medicine from Air Force C-17 transport planes. Not only was the U.S. helping innocent victims of the war, it also hoped to show the Muslim world that this was a war against terrorism, not Islam.

The food packets helped feed people in some of the most desperate camps, but there were so many refugees that air-drops alone could not supply them all. A land route would have to be opened so convoys could reach the refugees—and soon.

On the diplomatic front, bringing a more stable government to Afghanistan was a top U.S. priority once the Taliban had been thrown out. No longer could the U.S. neglect the region, as it had done after the Soviet withdrawal in 1989. If it was to make the area less appealing to terrorists, the U.S. needed a government in Afghanistan that was friendlier to American interests. But Afghanistan was under the control of several local warlords, who ruled over their own sections of the country. Some supported the Taliban, others did not. Getting them to work together, by setting aside ethnic hatred caused by decades of civil war, would be a major challenge.

Early in the war, there was talk of bringing back former Afghan King Mohamed Zahir Shah, who had been thrown out of power in 1973. Even though the 87-year-old king said he didn't want to rule again, he seemed willing to help create a new government.

Aiding refugees and setting up a U.S.-friendly government were good goals, but first the Taliban and al-Qaeda forces had to be dealt with. The United States was extremely reluctant to send in the massive numbers of troops needed to take over Afghanistan. One Pentagon study concluded that at least 100,000 troops would be needed in order to occupy and control the country. Leaders at the Pentagon, remembering the Soviet experience in Afghanistan, wanted to avoid taking territory and controlling it for long periods of time. They would instead rely on air strikes, and relatively small teams of Special Forces troops.

Hunting From Above

Crossing by air over the hills into Afghanistan from Tajikistan, U.S. soldiers keep watch from the open back end of a U.S. Army Special Forces Chinook helicopter.

The trouble with relying solely on air strikes is that the military can't occupy land, no matter how precise and powerful its bombs and missiles are. To grab territory, the military needed to use ground forces. The U.S. didn't have masses of troops in Afghanistan. But it *did* have the Northern Alliance.

The Northern Alliance was a group of rebel fighters that had been battling the Taliban for several years. Their stronghold was in the northeastern part of Afghanistan, and they held pockets of territory in the mountainous central region as well. Many Northern Alliance fighters were former *mujahideen* guerrillas who had fought the Soviets during the 1980s.

The Northern Alliance drew its support from ethnic groups within Afghanistan, including Tajik, Hazara, and Uzbek minorities. The Taliban, on the other hand, was made up mostly of Pashtun, the largest ethnic group in Afghanistan. They are concentrated mainly in the southern and eastern areas of the country. Drawing on this ethnic hostility, Pentagon planners would use the Northern Alliance to act as a proxy force, fighting on the ground for the United States. The U.S. and its allies in the war against terror, including Russia, began helping the Northern Alliance. The rebel group received fresh weapons, ammunition, and supplies, including heavy armor from Russia. They prepared for a new assault on the capital city of Kabul, or Mazar-e Sharif, a major city in north-central Afghanistan.

The U.S. plan began to take shape. Special Forces troops would be sent into Afghanistan. Once in place, they would disrupt Taliban forces with quick raids, and also collect as much information on al-Qaeda as possible. Most important, though, Special Forces soldiers would give accurate targeting information for air strikes. Once the air strikes destroyed Taliban forces, the Northern Alliance would sweep in, capturing the major cities and other vital areas of the country. The plan was risky. Could air strikes be effective against a country that had already suffered heavy damage from years of civil war? And could the Northern Alliance be relied upon to fight on the ground?

Air superiority gives a country a huge advantage on the battlefield, and the U.S. has worked hard to dominate the skies. The U.S. armed forces today have an amazing array of accurate bombs and missiles at their disposal. Some use Global Positioning System (GPS) receivers to guide themselves, while others, such as cruise missiles, use internal maps to find their way over the countryside to their targets. The most accurate targeting of all, however, is when a target is first "painted" by a laser beam. The missile steers itself toward the spot of light, hitting the target with great accuracy. There are several ways to paint a target, but the most reliable is when a soldier on the ground uses a special laser-targeting device.

Humanitarian Aid

Packets of food were air-dropped by U.S. planes to refugees in Afghanistan.

There are more than two million people in the U.S. military, but only 46,000 are Special Forces troops. Special Forces soldiers are elite, the cream of the crop. They are specially equipped with the best weapons available, and they have the advanced training to use them. They go on secret missions to some of the most hostile places on earth, and when they are successful, the world seldom hears about it. In any given week, about 5,000 Special Forces troops are in 60 countries around the globe, working on missions most of us will never learn about.

In the military, Special Forces are known as the "tip of the spear," the first to go into harm's way. In Afghanistan, groups of Special Forces troops were secretly sent into Taliban-controlled territory in late September. Commandos from Britain's elite Special Air Services were also sent to assist in the operation. By the first week of October, the U.S. military was in place and ready. President Bush gave the order to attack.

On October 7, 2001, waves of U.S. aircraft, plus American and British cruise missiles, filled the skies over Afghanistan. Navy F/A-18 and F-14 warplanes streaked in from aircraft carriers in the Arabian Sea, the Persian Gulf, and the Mediterranean Sea. B-52 and B-1B heavy bombers took off from the island of Diego Garcia in the Indian Ocean. Their loads of "dumb" bombs were used to decimate Taliban troops on the battlefield. B-2 stealth bombers flew from Whiteman Air Force Base in Kansas City, Missouri. They made the 7,200-mile trip nonstop, dropping precision-guided bombs with pinpoint accuracy.

The first Afghan targets were air defenses, airports, command centers, and training camps. The U.S. used powerful "bunker-buster" bombs to destroy underground barracks and headquarters. Laser-guided bombs wiped out Taliban tanks and other armored vehicles.

Some of the American precision-guided bombs fell off-target, causing civilian deaths. It's an unavoidable fact of warfare that innocent people are sometimes caught in the crossfire. However, most of the bombing was on-target, destroying Taliban forces without harming civilian structures nearby. Once U.S. Special Forces teams began painting targets with laser beams, the bombing became even more precise.

Within days, American aircraft owned the sky over Afghanistan. The next phase of the war was ready to begin.

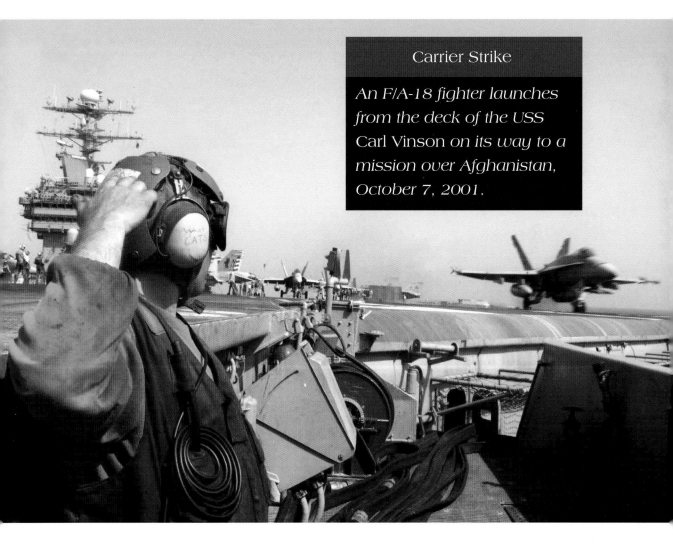

Carrier Strike

An F/A-18 fighter launches from the deck of the USS Carl Vinson on its way to a mission over Afghanistan, October 7, 2001.

Air Support

Afghan Northern Alliance fighters watch a U.S. air strike against Taliban troops.

Mazar-e Sharif

FOR MOST OF THE MONTH OF OCTOBER, THE U.S. continued a steady campaign of bombing fixed Taliban and al-Qaeda targets. Instead of bombing frontline Taliban troops, the U.S. concentrated first on resupply routes and reinforcements from the rear. The goal was to isolate enemy frontline troops and weaken them. Special Operations commandos were also busy gathering intelligence and disrupting the al-Qaeda network. In one case, the enemy tried to move ammunition and weapons in civilian moving vans. Green Beret teams called in air strikes, and U.S. aircraft promptly destroyed the vans.

The U.S. bombing strategy aimed to weaken the Taliban enough so that Northern Alliance troops, or defecting Taliban forces, could move in and take over. But frustration began to set in, especially among politicians in Washington, D.C. After a month of sustained bombing, the Taliban still controlled Afghanistan. The Northern Alliance refused to push forward. The war seemed to be at a stalemate, but planners at the Pentagon urged patience. They reassured the public that the bombing campaign would soon begin to pay off.

Taliban troops were massed near the two important cities of Kabul and Mazar-e Sharif. The Northern Alliance had been stalled near these areas, unable to push through the strong Taliban forces.

American B-52s began carpet-bombing Taliban troop positions with iron "dumb" bombs, cluster bombs, and 15,000-pound BLU-82 "daisy cutters." About the size of a small car, daisy cutters are the most powerful non-nuclear weapons in the U.S. arsenal. They can be deadly to anyone within 600 yards.

As if the bombing weren't enough, U.S. attack helicopters and AC-130 gunships entered the battle, shredding enemy troops and armor with devastating firepower. Special Forces troops helped pinpoint enemy targets for U.S. aircraft.

To the Taliban and al-Qaeda soldiers, who were used to fighting regular troops on a conventional battlefield, the American attacks were bewildering, and totally demoralizing. They couldn't shoot back at high-flying U.S. aircraft. Often they couldn't even see where the bombs and missiles were coming from. They could only huddle in their trenches, terrified of the unseen enemy that brought so much death from above.

By November 9, Northern Alliance forces finally pushed forward on their attack at Mazar-e Sharif. The Taliban panicked. Many fled their positions around the city. With help from U.S. Special Forces, the Northern Alliance overran the city within three days, even though they were outnumbered by Taliban forces. There was a terrible vengeance against Taliban and al-Qaeda fighters, especially against foreign Arabs who had come to fight for Osama bin Laden. They were viewed by the Afghan people as invaders, outsiders who had brought death and destruction to their country. Many al-Qaeda troops fought to the death. Hundreds more were killed by enraged Northern Alliance troops, even when they tried to surrender.

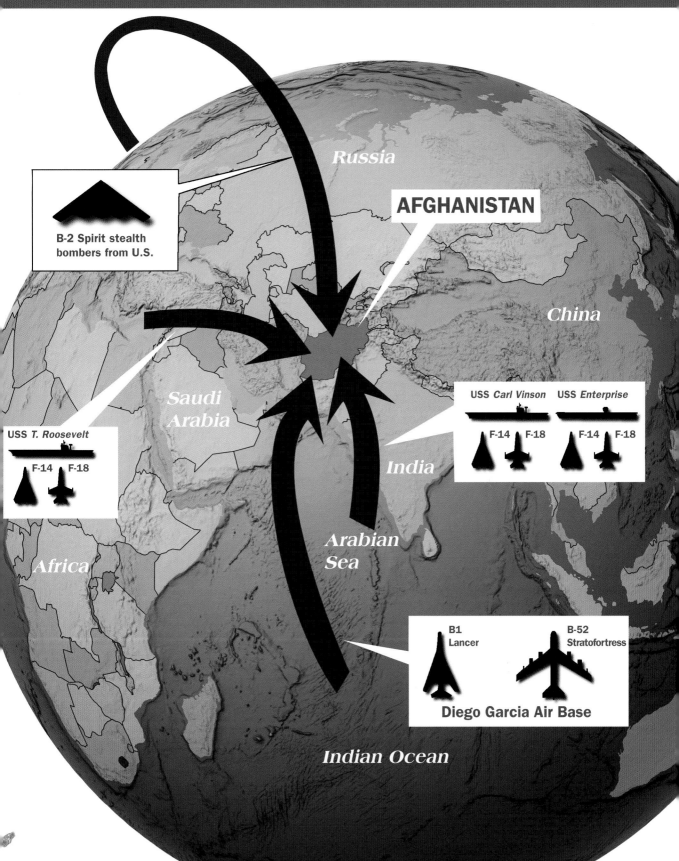

B-2 Spirit stealth bombers from U.S.

Russia

AFGHANISTAN

China

USS *Carl Vinson*   USS *Enterprise*

F-14   F-18   F-14   F-18

Saudi Arabia

India

USS *T. Roosevelt*

F-14   F-18

Arabian Sea

Africa

B1 Lancer

B-52 Stratofortress

Diego Garcia Air Base

Indian Ocean

In the city, joyful residents rushed into the streets, eager to greet their liberators. Now free from the strict rules of the Taliban, many men shaved their beards. Women began going out in public without their veils. People unearthed once-forbidden radios and televisions. Children flew kites once again.

With Mazar-e Sharif now free of the Taliban, United Nations relief convoys were soon able to begin delivering much-needed food and medicine to Afghan refugee camps in the north. With winter quickly approaching, the convoys came just in time, averting a major crisis.

The fall of Mazar-e Sharif was an important victory, but there was still much fighting to be done.

Hint Of Victory

Northern Alliance soldiers react with joy as Taliban troops are defeated.

High Tech, High Altitude

A U.S. Air Force B-1B Lancer makes a bombing run over Afghanistan.

Relentless Assault

Northern Alliance fighters use Soviet-made howitzers against Taliban positions.

The Taliban Collapse

WITH THE FALL OF MAZAR-E SHARIF, Taliban and al-Qaeda forces fled to the east, toward the city of Konduz, where they regrouped and then set up fortifications. The Arab al-Qaeda fighters were especially keen to make a last stand, to fight to the death.

Ignoring Konduz for the moment, Northern Alliance troops swept to the west and south, overrunning the city of Herat with the help of U.S. precision bombing and Special Forces. Outside the capital city of Kabul, U.S. air strikes intensified against dug-in Taliban troop positions. Some Taliban fighters tried to flee from the bombing by hiding in the many caves dotting the nearby hills that overlook the city. American "bunker-buster" bombs soon destroyed these positions. There was no place left for the Taliban to hide.

By November 13, Northern Alliance troops swarmed to the outskirts of Kabul, expecting fierce resistance. But most of the Taliban had already abandoned the city, fleeing to the south. They were heading to Kandahar in southern Afghanistan, the birthplace and last stronghold of the Taliban movement.

Despite political concerns, Northern Alliance forces found the undefended Kabul an irresistible target and swept in, occupying the city and liberating it from Taliban control. Almost at the same time, the eastern city of Jalalabad changed hands as local leaders rose up against Taliban forces. Except for the pocket of Taliban still holding out in Konduz, the entire northern half of the country was now under control of the rebels.

The speed of the Taliban's collapse took everyone by surprise. Many war planners at the Pentagon had expected to fight a much longer war, possibly through the winter and into the following spring. As one military analyst told the television news network CNN, "What normally causes such a collapse, as in Vietnam in 1975 and Iraq in 1991, is that forces lose hope. They realize they cannot talk, they cannot walk, they cannot resupply, and if they fight, they get killed. So they try to retreat to an area where they're able to regroup, which it appears the Taliban are doing toward Kandahar." Another factor in the sudden collapse was local people rising up and fighting the Taliban. After years of oppression, people were eager to join the fight for freedom.

Just two days after the fall of Kabul, U.S. aircraft began carpet-bombing holdout Taliban troops in the northern city of Konduz. By November 25, Northern Alliance forces claimed control of the city.

As the Northern Alliance swept through the country, U.S. forces continued a ferocious effort to hunt down Osama bin Laden and other al-Qaeda leaders. Several times, U.S. military intelligence identified al-Qaeda meeting places, which were laser-targeted by Special Forces or Predator drone aircraft flying overhead, and then bombed. Several top aids to bin Laden were killed, including Mohammed Atef, al-Qaeda's senior military planner.

By now, Taliban troops were surrendering or switching sides throughout Afghanistan. In the newly captured city of Mazar-e Sharif, several hundred Taliban prisoners were taken to a fortress-like prison on the outskirts of town. On November 25, a prisoner suddenly detonated a hidden hand grenade, while others grabbed weapons from surprised guards. The violent, three-day revolt was eventually stopped by U.S. air strikes and Northern Alliance troops, but hundreds of people were killed, including Johnny "Mike" Spann, an agent working for the U.S. Central Intelligence Agency (CIA). It was the first U.S. battle-related death of the war.

Switching Sides

Defecting Taliban fighters maneuver a tank through the front line near Konduz.

Meanwhile, in southern Afghanistan, U.S. planes staged relentless attacks on enemy soldiers in and around the city of Kandahar. Many of the remaining Taliban had retreated to the area and regrouped. Some vowed to make one last stand and fight to the death.

At a remote airstrip 70 miles south of the city, U.S. Marines set up Camp Rhino to use as a forward base of operation. Hundreds of Marines secured the base, and helicopter gunships were soon using it to launch strikes against enemy positions in the area. U.S. Navy and Air Force bombers continued their fierce bombing raids, and Northern Alliance forces encircled Kandahar, like a noose slowly tightening around the enemy. Local Pashtun also began rising up against the Taliban, increasing the pressure.

By the first week of December, Taliban troops began fleeing the city. Some surrendered, while others melted away into the mountains north of Kandahar. Many left with their weapons, perhaps to fight at a later time. As much as possible, U.S. forces hunted down these troops, trying to cut them off and prevent future trouble.

On December 7, Kandahar fell. The Taliban had lost the last major city under their control. As American and rebel forces entered the city, the leader of the Taliban, Mullah Mohammed Omar, was nowhere to be found. Most think he secretly fled Kandahar earlier, possibly finding shelter in the mountainous region to the north.

The speed of the Taliban collapse was breathtaking. It happened with a combination of air strikes, Special Forces intelligence gathering and target spotting, and the help of the Northern Alliance. This potent combination led to the Taliban's quick destruction. With its host country no longer in power, the al-Qaeda terror network was wounded and on the run.

Guard Duty

U.S. Marines stand ready in their foxholes at Camp Rhino in southern Afghanistan.

Tora Bora

AS ANTI-TALIBAN AND UNITED STATES Special Forces troops set to work mopping up pockets of enemy resistance in Afghanistan, the main focus of the U.S. effort turned to the eastern part of the country. Just south of the city of Jalalabad rise the forbidding peaks of the White Mountains. One section of these rugged mountains contains a stronghold known as Tora Bora, an area pockmarked with hundreds of caves. During the 1980s Soviet invasion, *mujahideen* rebels built a network of tunnels and underground hideouts in Tora Bora, sometimes with the help of the CIA. The caves withstood repeated bombing by Soviet forces.

During the 1990s, Osama bin Laden expanded these underground bunkers. Some were big enough to hide hundreds of troops, supplies, and tanks. With enough room for sleeping quarters, water and food supplies, and electrical generators, the cave complexes were self-sufficient enough for troops to hide out for a long time.

When the Taliban regime began to collapse, thousands of al-Qaeda fighters streamed into the Tora Bora area. U.S. officials suspected that Osama bin Laden, and possibly Mullah Mohammed Omar, were among those hiding out in the mountain fortress.

Hammering Tora Bora

An anti-Taliban soldier watches from his tank as U.S. fighter jets bomb al-Qaeda strongholds in the White Mountains.

During the first week of December, U.S. warplanes began a massive bombing campaign against the mountain lair, targeting above-ground al-Qaeda forces and underground complexes with a combination of laser-guided bunker busters, BLU-82 "daisy cutters," and AC-130 gunships. Many planes were equipped with infrared imaging sensors to make it easier to spot cave entrances and enemy troops hiding above ground.

The bombing lasted for several weeks, and was soon joined by U.S. Special Forces aiding anti-Taliban troops on the ground. In a series of fierce battles, the anti-Taliban forces hunted down al-Qaeda fighters cave by cave. Hundreds were killed. Many more fled south, toward the border with Pakistan, hoping to find refuge among rural villages friendly to the Taliban cause. American and Pakistani soldiers tried to seal the 1,510-mile (2,430-km) border, but the rugged terrain made it difficult to stop all the fleeing enemy forces. Many undoubtedly escaped.

By the end of December, most al-Qaeda soldiers had surrendered, been wiped out, or fled into the countryside. U.S. Special Forces scoured the remaining caves, searching for clues and gathering information about al-Qaeda operations. But the biggest question of all remained unanswered: where was Osama bin Laden?

An anti-Taliban fighter checks a cave used by al-Qaeda to store ammunition in Tora Bora.

Eyes On The Sky

An anti-Taliban soldier watches as U.S. jets pound Tora Bora.

On The Hunt

BY JANUARY 2002, THE UNITED STATES-LED war against terrorism in Afghanistan was winding down. To date, only two Americans had died in combat during Operation Enduring Freedom, although 17 others were killed in accidents. But Afghanistan was still a very dangerous place.

U.S. Special Forces continued rooting out pockets of Taliban and al-Qaeda fighters. Millions of hidden mines littered the countryside. Several ammunition dumps were discovered and destroyed. Many al-Qaeda fighters, including several top leaders, were rounded up and sent to holding facilities near Kandahar. Some were transferred to Camp X-Ray, a prison facility on the U.S. military base at Guantanamo Bay, Cuba.

Two people remained maddeningly elusive: Osama bin Laden and Mullah Mohammed Omar. The former Taliban supreme leader was thought to be in the mountains north of Kandahar, or perhaps seeking shelter in a neighboring province. If he is ever captured, he may face justice at the hands of a U.S. military tribunal.

Manhunt

U.S. Marines conduct a raid at a suspected al-Qaeda hideout in central Afghanistan.

As for bin Laden, his location was still a mystery. "We don't know where bin Laden is," said Army General Tommy Franks, commander in chief of U.S. Central Command. "We've been pretty honest about that. We've said he is either dead or alive, and he is either inside Afghanistan or he isn't."

Some believed bin Laden was hiding out with Omar in a remote region somewhere in central Afghanistan. Others guessed that he was ill, or that he had already died from sickness, possibly kidney failure. Others believed he died during the bombing of Tora Bora, or that if he survived he slipped across the border into Pakistan. If he did escape, there are few places in the world for bin Laden to hide. President Bush has vowed to hunt down the terrorist mastermind no matter how long it takes.

While the deadly manhunt continued, the business of rebuilding Afghanistan went on. A British-led peacekeeping force of about 2,500 troops was in Kabul, making sure that the streets were free from gun-toting street gangs, and that foreign embassies and Afghan government buildings remained secure. More peacekeepers would be added in the future, possibly expanding into other cities. The Afghan people feared more civil war. For now, they want foreign troops to remain in order to bring stability to the country.

Hamid Karzai, a skilled politician who seemed to have the support of most of the country, was leading the Afghan government. After a six-month period, a new government was to be created by a traditional Afghan meeting called *loya jirga*, or grand assembly. At the assembly, representatives from the various Afghan tribes or groups meet to discuss and resolve important matters. This political process is accepted and honored by the various ethnic and religious groups of Afghanistan.

Humanitarian Crisis

A mother clutches her child in the Mirkosymjan refugee camp, which houses nearly 4,000 families.

Shared Grief °

Hamid Karzai presents a memorial wreath at the World Trade Center, January 30, 2002.

In the period before the new government was to be created, Hamid Karzai lobbied the countries of the world for financial aid to rebuild Afghanistan. It's important for the U.S. to have a hand in Afghanistan's reconstruction. By supporting the new government, the United States shows its commitment to the region, and to keeping the forces of terrorism out for good.

On January 30, 2002, Hamid Karzai visited the site of the World Trade Center in New York City. He laid a wreath of yellow roses at the site and said that Afghanistan shares America's grief. "The Afghan people, they know the pain of the American people better than all other people," he said.

Earlier that week, Karzai had paid a state visit to the White House, in Washington, D.C., the first Afghan leader to do so since the 1960s. He was present when President George W. Bush gave his State of the Union speech before Congress on January 29, 2002.

In his speech, the president rallied the American people, and asked for their patience and determination. He also warned that "our war against terror is only beginning." But President Bush also expressed confidence that the war on terrorism would eventually succeed, thanks in large part to Operation Enduring Freedom and the skill of the U.S. armed forces. Said the president, "When I called our troops into action, I did so with complete confidence in their courage and skill. And tonight, thanks to them, we are winning the war on terror. The men and women of our armed forces have delivered a message now clear to every enemy of the United States: Even 7,000 miles away, across oceans and continents, on mountaintops and in caves, you will not escape the justice of this nation."

Warning To Terrorists

President Bush gives his State of the Union address at the Capitol in Washington, D.C., January 29, 2002.

Timeline

September 11, 2001	Terrorists use hijacked jets to attack the United States, damaging the Pentagon and destroying New York City's World Trade Center.
September 13, 2001	Secretary of State Colin Powell identifies Osama bin Laden as the prime suspect in the terror attacks.
September 15, 2001	President George W. Bush orders the U.S. military to prepare for war against terrorism. Four days later, ships, planes, and troops are sent to Afghanistan.
October 7, 2001	Waves of American planes, plus U.S. and British cruise missiles, begin pounding Taliban positions within Afghanistan.
November 9, 2001	After weeks of intense American bombing, Northern Alliance forces on the ground capture the northern city of Mazar-e Sharif.
November 13, 2001	Northern Alliance forces march into the capital city of Kabul, for the most part unopposed by fleeing Taliban troops.
November 25, 2001	After a massive U.S. bombing effort, the Northern Alliance captures the city of Konduz, the last Taliban stronghold in the northern part of Afghanistan.
December 7, 2001	Kandahar, the last major Taliban-controlled city in Afghanistan, falls after U.S. bombing and military pressure on the ground from the Northern Alliance.
December 2001	Intense U.S. bombing of Tora Bora, the al-Qaeda stronghold in the mountainous northeast part of Afghanistan. Surviving al-Qaeda forces flee by the end of the month.
January 30, 2002	Interim Afghan leader Hamid Karzai visits the site of World Trade Center in New York City. He lays a memorial wreath in memory of victims of terrorism.

Where On The Web?

http://www.terrorism.com/index.shtml
The official site of the Terrorism Research Center is dedicated to informing the public of the phenomena of terrorism and information warfare. The site features essays and thought pieces on current issues, as well as links to other terrorist documents, research, and resources.

http://www.af.mil/
Official site of the U.S. Air Force. Excellent selection of photos, artwork, and diagrams, plus news stories.

http://www.army.mil/
Official site of the U.S. Army.

http://www.navy.mil/
Official site of the U.S. Navy.

http://www.usmc.mil/
Official site of the U.S. Marine Corps.

http://www.defenselink.mil/pubs/almanac/
Defense Almanac is a site filled with facts and statistics about the United States Department of Defense.

Glossary

casualty
A person who is injured or killed in an act of war.

combat air patrol
A patrol of fighter aircraft stationed over an area (usually a military task force) that destroys enemy aircraft threatening to attack.

democracy
A government by the people that is ruled by the majority through representation involving free elections.

early warning radar
Sophisticated radar that detects when enemy planes are entering friendly territory. In war, it is common practice to first destroy early warning radar sites so that the air force can then fly missions with a greater element of surprise.

Pentagon
The huge, five-sided building near Washington, D.C., where the main offices of the U.S. Department of Defense are located.

reconnaissance
Finding the location of the enemy. "Recon" missions help commanders decide which forces to send into enemy territory.

smart bomb

A bomb or missile that navigates its way to a target, usually by following a laser beam "painted" on the target by a plane or special operations soldier on the ground. Smart bombs are usually very accurate.

weapons of mass destruction

Weapons that kill or injure large numbers of people, or cause massive damage to buildings. When people talk about weapons of mass destruction, they are usually referring to nuclear, biological, or chemical weapons.

Let's Roll

A U.S. Marine prepares to go on patrol in Afghanistan.

Index